High School Musicals™

DANCE and CHOREOGRAPHY

rosen publishing's
rosen central®
New York

Michael Joosten

To Gaye Humphrey, Stephen Terrell, and Marlena Yannetti,
who gave me the support and opportunities to feel like a Baryshnikov,
instead of a bozo

Published in 2010 by The Rosen Publishing Group, Inc.
29 East 21st Street, New York, NY 10010

Library of Congress Cataloging-in-Publication Data

Joosten, Michael.
Dance and choreography / Michael Joosten.—1st ed.
    p. cm.—(High school musicals)
Includes bibliographical references and index.
ISBN-13: 978-1-4358-5261-7 (library binding)
ISBN-13: 978-1-4358-5536-6 (pbk)
ISBN-13: 978-1-4358-5537-3 (6 pack)
1. Dance—Juvenile literature. 2. Choreography—Juvenile literature.
I. Title.
GV1596.5.J68 2010
792.8—dc22

                                                    2008046812

Manufactured in Malaysia

Contents

Introduction   4

CHAPTER 1
The Audition   6

CHAPTER 2
The Rehearsal   21

CHAPTER 3
Opening Night   34

CHAPTER 4
After Your Performance   45

Glossary   55

For More Information   57

For Further Reading   60

Bibliography   61

Index   62

INTRODUCTION

Bob Fosse once said, "The time to sing is when your emotional level is too high to just speak anymore, and the time to dance is when your emotions are just too strong to only sing about how you feel." When we think of methods of communication onstage, speaking and singing are what most commonly come to mind because they are verbal tools. However, nonverbal communication can be just as—if not more effective than—using words. Witnessing someone express fear, love, joy, sadness, or any other emotion through dance can be an incredibly moving experience for a performer and his or her audience, and that is exactly your job when dancing. It is up to you to take your audience along on the journey of your story.

Your participation in a high school musical can give you that opportunity. Whether you hope to turn that experience into a

This group of male dancers from the musical *West Side Story* perform in dress rehearsal for a Broadway tribute in New York.

career or simply want to see if you enjoy the theater, a high school musical is an ideal way to make new friends, branch out of your comfort zone, and experience the feeling of being onstage. It's an environment where you are given the ability to create, to work as a team, and to grow as an individual. It's an environment that will test your endurance and your commitment—in the best ways possible.

CURTAIN UP!

The Audition

The ability to tell a story or heighten an action through any genre of dance is a unique and riveting combination. Whether it is ballet, modern, jazz, tap, or hip-hop, all styles of dance are individually powerful. This is why dancing in musical theater is such a unique experience; it is one of the few mediums where these styles are allowed to fuse together. Some of the most successful and acclaimed musical theater choreography of all time is a direct result of the blending of alternate styles of dance. Knowledge of these different styles will only enhance your ability to execute them in your auditions, rehearsals, and performances. Let's take a look at some different styles of dance.

- Ballet is considered to be the most formal style of dance. It is extremely technical, with an emphasis placed on skills that include pointe work, turnout, placement, flexibility, and grace.

- Jazz dance, according to Matt Mattox, an acclaimed choreographer, is "a skillful combination of rhythm and design." This style of dance emphasizes syncopation, individual style, and improvisation. In addition, connecting with the music is key because jazz dance directly expresses the mood of the music that the steps are set to.
- Modern dance originated as a rebellion of ballet, and as opposed to jazz, modern dance is not as dependent upon the beats of the music matching the movements. Its emphasis is on creative self-expression, rather than technical precision. Different postures, character movements, and an emphasis on the individual body are all components of modern dance.
- Tap dance is a style that involves specific rhythmical patterns of foot movement that create a tapping sound. The unique thing about tap dancing is that the dancer also acts as a type of musician. The taps created by the dancer serve as percussion for the piece.

Preparing for Your Audition

One of the greatest ways in which you can help prepare yourself for your dance audition is to take dance classes. If you have limited experience with dance, enrolling in several beginner classes will give you opportunities to get basic training under your belt before the big day. Due to musical theater's heavy emphasis on the jazz style, a jazz class would be the most beneficial in terms of what style you would most likely be doing in the actual show. However, as ballet is considered the foundation of dance, you may want to enroll in a few beginner ballet classes in order to learn the basics of dance technique as well. You will most likely

A group of young teens rehearses a jazz combination. Their movement includes a step called a passe, where the foot is brought parallel to the opposite knee.

be able to find a dance studio in your area. Call around and find out about the class schedules. Ask a friend to take the class with you!

You may also want to research the actual show your high school will be performing as soon as you find out what it will be.

The style of the show will directly affect the style of choreography that will be used. Therefore, there are several components you should investigate in order to gain a better understanding of what you will be performing.

Sometimes, a show you are performing will have a filmed version or performance version available—a taping of an actual theatrical performance. If you are unfamiliar with the show, getting a copy could help a lot. Although your high school's production will be different from the filmed version—since high school musicals tend not to have multimillion-dollar Hollywood budgets—you can still gain an understanding of the overall feel and roles of the show.

Your high school or local library may also have original cast recordings available on CD. You should find a copy of the CD as soon as you find out what the show will be. Familiarizing yourself with the music can enhance your understanding of how it works within the show. It may also give you a leg up on the competition, as some choreographers tend to use music directly from the show for auditions.

In a ballet class, dancers pay close attention to the alignment of their heads. Posture and clean lines are two of the staples of ballet technique.

Emotions

Auditions are one of the few experiences that encompass a wide range of emotions in a short period of time. You may experience excitement, fear, courage, or pride, and a combination of these can feel a bit overwhelming. Therefore, the first thing you should keep in mind when going to any audition is that the judges are not rooting against you. They want you to have fun and succeed at what you are doing. Be yourself! Judges want to see talented performers bring their vision of the show to life.

Dressing for Your Audition

For your audition, be sure to wear the required clothing. It's the first indication to the director and choreographer that you know how to take direction. More than likely, you will be told what to wear in the audition notice. However, if it doesn't say, contact whoever is organizing the audition and ask him or her what the dress code will be. You're already starting on the right foot by ensuring that you will meet the judges' standards of dress even before walking in the door. As a general guideline, you may want to follow the standard dress code below.

Girls

Hair should be pulled back from the face. The judges want to be able to see you, and hair can easily fall into your eyes and mouth once the choreography begins.

A leotard in a solid color and black tights are ideal. Feel free to throw on a pair of jazz shorts as well. Some dancers prefer a bright memorable color that will stand out among the other dancers. Others prefer a dark color that shows off the lines the body will be creating. Whatever you choose should be flattering to your figure. You can purchase these clothes at your local dance store.

The shoe requirements may vary. You may be asked for traditional jazz shoes (black sneakers) or character shoes (low heels). Either can be purchased at your local dance store or online.

Be sure to remove all your jewelry. The intensity of the choreography can cause jewelry to distract the judges, not to mention a hassle for you if it falls off.

Minor makeup is fine. However, be sure you don't overdo it. You'll be sweating in the audition, and makeup and water are not a good mix.

Do not wear perfume. It's best to keep smells neutral in rehearsal because sweat can change the scents of the perfume.

Boys

Hair can be worn any way. However, if it is long, it's best to tie it back in order to keep it from your eyes.

A dark-colored tank top or fitted T-shirt and dark athletic warm-up pants (solid colors are best) should get you through any audition. These can be purchased at a local dance or sporting goods store.

Jazz shoes (black sneakers) will be your footwear requirement. These, too, can be purchased at your local dance store.

Be sure to remove all your jewelry (earrings, necklaces, and rings). Some of the choreography may cause the jewelry to fall off, and that will detract attention from the audition. You want the judges to focus on you, not your "bling."

Do not wear cologne.

Now, if you remember any part of this chapter, please let it be this invaluable piece of advice: Wear deodorant! You will be firing on all cylinders and sweating. Body odor is your personal enemy. Fight it with deodorant.

The Day of Your Audition

When you arrive at the audition, there should be a sign-in sheet. Typically, once you sign in, you will be given a sticker with a number on it to place on your clothing so that the judges can identify you. Though a sticker isn't exactly fashionable, it's best to place it front and center so that the judges can see it. Once you have signed in and have your number, it's time to start preparing your mind and body for the choreography you'll be given to perform.

One of the best ways to help center yourself and not feel so anxious is to remember to breathe. It sounds simple, but it's one of the first things people forget to do in an audition. When nerves start to

In order to stretch her hamstring and practice arm positioning, this ballet dancer places her foot on the ballet barre and performs a "port de bras."

take over, your breathing becomes shallow and you may not inhale to your full capacity. These shallow breaths will only increase the feeling of nervousness. Therefore, take a few deep breaths that you can feel in your diaphragm. We've all had the feeling of butterflies in our stomachs, and deep breaths will help alleviate some of them. Whenever you start to feel nervous throughout the audition, breathe.

Learning the Choreography

Now, it is time to learn the choreography. The choreographer will ask you to line up behind him or her. You'll want to stand somewhere

Warm-Ups

At this point, you will also want to start warming up your body so that it can perform at maximum capacity. You want to get your muscles warm and your senses sharpened. Here are some good warm-ups to help achieve that.

Slowly roll your head from the right, to the front, and to the left. Then, reverse directions. Three times each way should be sufficient.

Lift your arms over your head to stretch the upper half of your body. Then, take your left arm and reach over your head to the right so that the left side of your rib cage feels a good stretch. Next, reach your right arm over your head to the left so that you feel the same stretch in your right side.

Lean forward, but keep your back straight like a tabletop. This will help stretch your hamstrings and calf muscles.

Sit on the floor with your legs in a V-shape. Lean forward and place your hands on the floor while trying to keep your back straight. This fully stretches the hamstrings. While you do this stretch, point and flex your feet and wiggle your toes. You want to wake those up, too.

Remember not to stretch to the point where it hurts. Warm-ups should feel good. You don't want to injure yourself before your audition!

in the room where you have a view of the choreographer. Auditions can be intimidating, and hiding in the back may seem comfortable, but if you do, you might miss some of the steps. Don't worry about the people behind you or feel insecure. Focus on the choreographer.

You first will be taught the steps without the music. The choreographer will do this with counts, "One, two, three, four, five, six, seven,

Students in a hip-hop class rehearse their high-energy routine that includes body locks and body breaks. These types of moves are individual isolations of portions of the dancer's body.

eight." These counts are like a cheat sheet for the steps. Each one will tell you which position or in what direction your body needs to travel. The only thing you need to do is remember which movement goes with which count. This can get tricky, especially when the music is added. However, determine which steps you know you'll remember, and then focus on the ones that you know will be trouble spots for

you. Feel free to raise your hand and ask a question if you are unclear. The choreographer will be happy to clarify. In addition, if you are in the back row, raise your hand and ask if it's OK to "switch lines." This is when the front line moves to the back and the back line moves to the front. That way, you can get a view from the front as well.

At this point, you will be divided into small groups to perform the choreography. Be careful not to depend on the other people in your group to know the steps. Following the steps of the person in front of you isn't always a good way to remember the routine. If that person misses a step, you will probably miss the step as well.

Focus on what sets you apart from the other people you are auditioning with. The best way to get the judges to notice your ability is to show your personality when you dance. It's not just about executing the steps. Flawless steps aren't what make a dancer interesting to watch. It's the personality the individual incorporates with those steps that makes him or her someone people will notice. Smile, bring energy to the movements, and have fun. Missing a step can be forgiven easily if you have personality to carry you through it.

After your audition is over, it is natural to continuously replay events in your mind. "How did I look?" "The person next to me was so much better." "If only I had nailed that one turn!" Everyone that you auditioned with is probably thinking exactly the same things. This is completely natural. Try not to obsess about them. Auditions create enough anxiety, so don't make more by worrying when it's actually over. Allow yourself to feel proud if you did a good job. If it didn't go as well as you would have liked, it's not the end of the world. There will be other auditions for other shows. That one audition does not mean that you are the world's most talented dancer, nor does it mean that you are the world's worst. It is only a reflection of how you did in that one audition, in that one moment, on that one day.

The Show's Choreographer

If you're already an experienced dancer who has spent some time on the stage, there is a chance that the director may ask you to be the show's choreographer. In this event, there will be similarities between your preparation and that of the people who will be auditioning for you. The first thing you will need to do is have a production meeting with the director. In this meeting, you need to get a sense of the director's vision of the show. Will he or she be changing the time period or the setting? What themes will be emphasized? Is anything being done to alter the roles featured in the show? These components will serve as an indicator of what your choreography will need to be. For example, if the director decides that he or she wants to move the time period of the show from the 1920s to the 1970s, you may want to incorporate elements of disco into the choreography. After asking the director any questions that you may have, you will want to begin creating a combination to teach at the audition. This will help you see the varying skill levels of the people who are trying out. Here are some things to keep in mind:

Although you are not required to set the combination to the music featured in the production, doing so will allow you to get a true feeling of what these individuals will look like performing with the score of the show.

When creating the routine that will be used for the audition, keep in mind that it is best to choreograph moves in eight-count steps. That particular rhythm is easiest to teach. Begin by creating one eight-count. Keep in mind that the audition length will most likely be limited. Therefore, get right into the style of what you are hoping to see within the first set of counts. Your second set of eight-counts should build from your first set. Make sure that each set flows effortlessly into one another. Continue adding eight-count steps until your choreography includes everything that you are hoping to see from those auditioning. However, the eight-counts should not exceed the length of the song.

Be aware that people attending the audition will have varying skill levels of dance. Therefore, you should incorporate different levels into your routine. Make sure that the less experienced dancers are given something that will challenge them, while still allowing them the opportunity to showcase their potential. For the more advanced dancers, you will want to include some moves with increased technical demands—such as double pirouettes or leaps—so that you get a feel for what increasingly elaborate moves you can incorporate into your choreography.

Now, whether you are the choreographer who is putting on the audition or the dancer who is about to audition, you are ready for the audition portion of your high school musical.

The Rehearsal

What happens in the rehearsal process is what will determine the quality of performance you bring to the stage. Being focused, professional, and prepared will help ensure your confidence in the choreography and how to best deliver it to your audience. As intimidating as those three components can sound, utilizing them will also help make your rehearsals fun and productive, and that is when your best work can happen.

The First Day of Rehearsal

You never truly know what will be on the schedule for the first day of rehearsal. But the one thing you can expect is to hit the ground running. Typically, your rehearsal time will be limited to after school and on weekends. Therefore, the choreographer will want to start teaching you the material right away. It can be overwhelming, and there may be some steps that don't come naturally to you. Do not

A choreographer works with a group of young girls in order to teach them how to incorporate a tricky prop (the umbrellas) into their routine.

get discouraged. The choreographer saw what you were capable of in your audition and would not have wanted you in the show unless he or she thought you could handle the steps. If you start to feel yourself getting frustrated, remember to breathe and relax. If you can't make sense of the step in that moment, you eventually will

be able to after some practice. Feel free to ask the choreographer a question, and go over your steps at home or before school with your cast mates or even during lunch. The more comfortable you are with the moves, the better your performance will be.

One of the best parts about being in a high school musical is that you will most likely have friends in your cast. This can make the long rehearsal hours more bearable because it's an experience you are sharing with people you are close to. However, those long rehearsal hours and drama from a long day at school can make everyone a little testy. Therefore, you have to enter each rehearsal with "clean feet." Just like wiping your feet on a mat before entering a home, you have to leave all your "drama" on the doorstep of your rehearsal space. No matter what issues you may have with friends or fellow cast mates, you must always agree on one thing: making the best show possible.

Sometimes, it won't be your cast mates that frustrate you—it can actually turn out to be the choreographer. There may be times when you may not see eye-to-eye with him or her. You may disagree with the choice of dancers for a specific number. You may feel that the choreographer favors particular people in your cast over others. There could be a time when you think the choreography isn't as exciting or inventive as you hoped it would be. You may be right about any or all of these things! However, always remember that you have been cast to take direction from the choreographer, not give it. Unless the choreographer asks a specific question of you, respect his or her choices.

Effort and Enthusiasm

Another thing that can bring you success during rehearsals is an ability to be "on" during them, or giving every step all your effort. Sometimes, it can be difficult after a long day at school to rehearse for several more hours. However, you have to summon your energy and make sure that you are rehearsing at your peak capability. Sometimes, the choreographer will tell you to "mark" the number. This means that you don't have to perform it at the level you would during the actual show. But unless the choreographer gives you that option, you want to be sure that you are firing on all cylinders. Choreographers take note of who is working hard during their rehearsals. They want to see your energy and commitment in their steps, and if they see you providing that, your chances of being featured in the show will greatly increase.

Two hip-hop dancers show that one of the key ingredients to a successful routine is not only energy, but a lively connection with your audience.

Preparations for the Choreographer

If you are the show's choreographer, preparing for the beginning of rehearsals may seem like a daunting and overwhelming task. At times, it will be exactly that. However, there are a variety of approaches you can take while creating your choreography that will help keep you on task and on schedule.

Make sure you have great deal of familiarity with the music in the show. Be sure to meet with the musical director to make sure that there are no special cuts or extra measures. One of the most frustrating things for a choreographer is to create a dance, only to find out that there are extra counts or the song has actually been cut to create a shorter version.

Choreograph the group numbers first. Teaching group numbers can be difficult due to the different skill levels of your ensemble. They are also the hardest numbers to change because of the number of people involved in them.

When it comes time to choreograph the smaller numbers, consider which character is speaking and what the song is about. Is the dance a romantic moment between a couple, or is it a playful scene with four friends? It will make your job easier if, from the very beginning of your creative process, you determine the mood of the piece and the number of people that will be needed for the number.

Taking Charge

Your first rehearsal, as choreographer, is your opportunity to set the tone of how you will be running things. Given the fact that you are a student choreographer, you will be working with your peers. It is important to let them know that you are all in this together, but you

Packing a Dance Bag

The night before your first day of rehearsal, you will want to pack a dance bag. This will act as your survival kit for those long hours of singing, dancing, and acting. Inside of it, you will want to include the required clothing (what you wore to the audition should suffice), but you should also include a few other things as well:

- A bottle of water. Who knows if the water fountain will be working—or if there even is one!
- Hand towel. You're going to be sweating, whether you want to or not.
- Deodorant. No explanation needed.

Rehearsals are typically long. So, you will want to bring food, such as carrot sticks, apples, and snack bars, that will fuel your body for all that will be required of it.

- Knee pads. The choreography may include some work on the floor, and you will want to protect your knees while first learning the steps.
- Snack. Toss an apple or carrot sticks in your bag. If you get a break, they are a quick source of fuel that will not make you feel too stuffed when you have to start dancing again.

also have a job to do and would like to set some ground rules in order for rehearsals to run smoothly:

Performers must be on time to all rehearsals. One missing dancer can cause a gap in the layout of the choreography. This can make it difficult to get the numbers to gel correctly and becomes frustrating for the cast members that are present. Emphasize the importance of each member of the production. For the benefit of the show, everyone must be at rehearsals on time.

There should be no talking while you are teaching. Even though these people are around your age, you deserve the same amount of respect that would be given to an outside choreographer.

Stress the importance of the rehearsal dress code. It allows performers maximum mobility and comfort during the long rehearsal hours.

Tell your ensemble that not all the casting for the numbers has been completed. Let them know that people who you see are working hard are more likely to be added to more numbers. This allows the cast to know that upping their game and being "on" at all times will work to their advantage.

Setting a Warm-Up Routine

At the beginning of rehearsal, be sure to lead the cast in a warm-up. Warm-up exercises help to raise body temperature, increase blood flow, and make muscles ready for the demands of the dancing ahead. A good jazz warm-up prepares your body to dance. It should not make you sweat or feel exhausted. It should raise your body temperature and heart rate to a "working" rate.

Blood needs to be flowing, airways need to be open, and muscles need to be given plenty of oxygen. Remember to start out small and gradually increase motion and range. A pulled muscle is

A ballet dancer demonstrates the amount of grace and elegance of that particular style by paying very close attention to her body posture during this warm-up exercise.

actually a tear in a muscle or tendon that was not properly warmed up for what was required of it. Add movement specific to the style of dance you are choreographing with. For example, a ballet warm-up will include pliés, while tap dancers will practice various shuffles.

You will want to be sure that every member of the company is participating. Make sure that the warm-up is fairly uniform day to day. The more familiar the dancers are with your warm-up, the more they can focus on preparing their minds and bodies for your rehearsal. Following the warm-ups, explain your goals for that particular rehearsal. When everyone is aware of the tasks at hand—and feels responsible for accomplishing them—you create a camaraderie beneficial to the productivity of your rehearsals.

Time Management

As choreographer, it is your responsibility to utilize rehearsal time to the maximum capacity. There is nothing more unproductive and frustrating for your dancers than sitting on the sidelines while you teach another part of the cast a new dance. Therefore, your best option is to make sure that your rehearsal space has an additional room where you can send dancers who aren't being used in the number you are teaching. A separate space provides an area for dancers to practice or polish some of the other numbers from the show. Ask a member of the cast to be a leader and run over a number with his or her cast mates. This gives dancers the opportunity to brush up on, or even improve, a specific number, while you concentrate on other matters.

Understandably, the more your dancers review a number, the more comfortable they will become with it. Therefore, you should view each rehearsal as an evolution of the previous one. Think about what it is that you would like to see out of your ensemble as the timeline of your rehearsals marches on. The following are some tips to help you manage your rehearsal time effectively:

- When teaching the choreography for the first time, make sure that your dancers feel comfortable asking questions. The first time they are learning the steps will serve as the foundation for the entire number. You can prevent future confusion by taking a few minutes to answer questions at the beginning.

- During the third rehearsal of any given number, you should ask your cast to begin to incorporate elements of their characters into the choreography. Nobody enjoys watching performers dance just for the sake of dancing. What makes it interesting is the characterization that dancers bring to what they are doing. Talk to them about what this specific dance represents in the show. If it's supposed to be a rip-roaring ensemble number, they need to bring rip-roaring characterization to the dance.

- When the technical steps are understood and the characterization work is incorporated, you should have the cast perform the number as if it were the actual show. Tell them that you want to see performance-level energy and emotion. If you run the number and don't feel like you are seeing what you expect from them, have them do it until it reaches the expected performance level. Although this might not make the cast very happy, it will help them understand the level of energy you need or the direction in which you want the number to travel. On opening night, you will be glad you were tough!

Dancers rehearse a large group number for their show. They prove that even though they are only in rehearsal, the effort they are putting into it is at a performance level.

Before the end of each rehearsal, you should run the number or numbers you have worked on that day. Be sure and take notes while you are watching. This will serve as a reminder for what you feel needs to be cleaned up. Your notes should also include specific things you would like to tell an individual dancer or the entire cast.

If you feel someone isn't giving his or her all, make a note that says you would like to see more energy from that person. If someone is doing amazing, write exactly that. If you feel the group needs to bring more characterization to the moves, be sure to include that in what you're writing. About fifteen minutes before the end of rehearsal, share these notes with your cast. These notes are not criticisms, so be sure to tell the ensemble that the things you are addressing will only serve to bring the show to a higher level of excellence.

Opening Night

Congratulations! You've made it past the anxiety of your audition and through the long hours of rehearsal. And now, the most enjoyable part of your high school musical is about to happen—opening night! You are about to experience something that few other people ever will—the power to take an audience outside of their daily lives and into a world where song and dance are the ultimate method of expression. That journey starts as soon as that curtain rises.

Most important, you must also prepare your body to perform, and a thorough warm-up is key! You and the other cast members may want to warm up as a group. Everyone should begin to warm up about forty-five minutes before the start of the show. Elect one person to lead the warm-up. Try the warm-up featured in the first chapter. Not only does this get the entire cast prepared physically, but it's also a great way to begin to completely focus on the task at hand.

A duo waits in the wings for their cue to take the stage on the opening night of their show. This is the moment they have been working for!

Dealing with Your Fears

A common fear for most performers is that you will forget part of the dance while you are onstage. At times, you may even be having these thoughts while in the middle of the actual number. It is very common to get caught up in "How am I doing?" while the actual

Eager performers hit the stage and demonstrate that they are ready for their musical's upcoming opening night by executing a dress rehearsal after weeks of preparation and dedication.

show is going on. Having your friends and family in the audience can make you feel self-conscious. Therefore, it is up to you to focus and think only about your character and the world of the show. This anxiety is something that even professionals feel. More than likely, you will be fine and remember everything. You have been rehearsing a great deal and should trust that the choreography is now second nature to you.

However, in the unlikely event that you do miss a step, take a slight spill, or miss an entrance, don't panic. Panicking will only make it more difficult to get back on track with the rest of the number. Once you have mentally processed that, yes, you may have done something that you are not thrilled with, realize that there is still more of the number to perform. The best option you have is to jump right back into the dance with a smile on your

face and act as if nothing happened. The audience may not have even noticed. Even if they did, they will be impressed that you picked yourself up, dusted yourself off, and jumped right back into the choreography. Though performance fears are natural and will be present at times, you must be as fearless as possible.

Without a doubt, you will be nervous before you go onstage. You might experience fear, excitement, or a combination of the two. Opening-night jitters are a natural part of the theater, so know that they are normal and expected. Use nervousness to your advantage. You will have adrenaline running through your body, and that can be useful for a performance. You actually have the control to harness that adrenaline and focus it into something useful, instead of allowing it to hinder you. You have put many hours of rehearsal into this show and, as a result, know the choreography, even if you are having a panic attack backstage thinking that you won't remember any of it. Therefore, trust that these jitters are good nerves in disguise and use them to propel the energy of your performance.

As a performer, you are constantly having to take risks. You are putting yourself in the vulnerable position of having people watch you onstage! However, you have to trust your abilities and know that you have something that makes you unique and valuable. This line of thought will not only help you artistically but personally as well. Dance can exist as a form of enjoyment, stress relief, or freedom, and all of these things can be experienced on a stage. Therefore, don't think about the doubts that you may be feeling. Dancing is about movement. You don't move with your mind; you move with your body. So, don't let your mind get in the way.

Also, remember that the performance is the result of your entire cast and crew working together. Your director, choreographer, costume designer, set designer, lighting designer, and backstage crew are all intricate and invaluable components of the show you

Costume Changes

Chances are, you will have at least one costume change during the show. These changes can come at a fast and furious pace. You may have less than thirty seconds to change an entire outfit before having to dart back onstage for the following number.

When you arrive at the theater, the first thing you should do is "pre-set" your costume or costumes. This means that you need to decide what location offstage is best for changing in the amount of time you have before you are needed back onstage. By creating this game plan, you will develop a rhythm in your costume changes, helping you make your entrances on time. Be sure to communicate with the stage manager and wardrobe head. It is part of their jobs to help your costume changes run smoothly.

are about to perform. That is a lesson that even some professionals tend to forget. It doesn't matter if you have a lead or are in the ensemble, if you are working backstage or are an usher for the house. It takes each one of you to get the show to come together and run. You are all in this together.

Opening-Night Prep for the Choreographer

A few weeks before the curtain goes up, you will want to start run-throughs of the show. This is when you perform the show from start to finish—without an audience—in order to get a feel for its timing, smooth out any problem spots, and see if any numbers need tweaking. During the run-through, you should make sure to have pad and pen in hand so that you can take notes about what you are seeing. There are two major things you will want to pay close attention to.

Stage Traffic Patterns

In order to have seamless numbers, paying close attention to stage traffic patterns is key. Seeing as how dance is movement, your ensemble will obviously be moving around the stage during the numbers. Therefore, during the run-through, keep an eye out for

High school students strut their stuff in a dance sequence from their production. They show that working well together as an ensemble results in a better show.

places where dancers may collide. Their safety is the number-one priority. If something in the choreography feels too close for comfort, you may need to reassess that portion and substitute another set of counts. Try to notice if someone is unable to make it from one location to another because of crowding. Typically, it can be easily solved when the whole cast is made aware of the

situation. If the performer cannot safely make it from point A to point B, have your dancers work together to create a bit of a path. By simply making them aware that someone will be tearing across the stage, they will be sure not to be in the way. In addition, on the first day you are allowed to do a run-through on the stage, you should have a mark-through of all the dances. This will allow your dancers to adapt to their new space and begin to anticipate possible glitches before the first complete run-through on the stage.

Seeing as how your show is nearing its opening night, you should continue to take notes and talk to your cast about what you are seeing. At this point, your ensemble will be at performance level in terms of the actual steps and individual characterizations. However, now that they have moved from the rehearsal space to the stage, you may see issues that you haven't yet encountered, such as:

- **Spacing** Now that your cast is in the actual performance space, you will most likely have to make adjustments to the spacing of the dancers. If you find that you have empty portions of the stage that you would like filled, have the cast take their places for the particular number that you would like to fix. While they wait in their positions, move out into the house and get a full view of the stage and your ensemble. Then, note who needs to move and where they need to move. It's a lot like moving chess pieces around a chessboard!

- **Energy** Although you will have discussed energy with your cast during rehearsal, you may need to have the discussion again once you've transitioned to the stage. The difference in the sizes of the rehearsal space and the performance space will be large. Therefore, what reads as powerful and energetic in one space may not read like that in another. Talk to your cast about making the execution and energy of the moves even more precise and powerful. Choreography has to be seen and felt all the way to the last row of the theater.

These four dancers are making final preparations for opening night by discussing last-minute suggestions from the director and choreographer.

- **Costumes** Another component that you will want to play close attention to will be the incorporation of costumes. You will find that certain costumes can make a dance more difficult for your performer. If you have someone in a pair of pants with little elasticity and his or her movement is grand battements, there is a good chance that the pants will rip or that the effectiveness of the move will be completely lost. Therefore, the sooner you can start rehearsing with the costumes, the better. Schedule a meeting with the costume designer and director right after the show is cast to talk about fabric and design options.

When opening night arrives, you will be able to just sit back and watch your dancers perform. You have guided your ensemble of dancers from learning the very first steps of your work in a rehearsal space all the way to showtime on the actual stage! Before the curtain goes up, gather the director and the entire cast together onstage. This is an ideal time to express your appreciation for all the hard work and long hours your dancers put in. They will, without a doubt, be dealing with nerves at this time, so use this opportunity to encourage and reassure them as well. You have seen their work and you know the show is in excellent hands (and feet). Now, enjoy the show!
PLACES, EVERYONE!

After Your Performance

The performance is over and you have taken your bow. So, what happens now? Maybe you want to use your experience in high school musicals as a springboard to a professional career in the theater. Or, perhaps you would just like to continue to participate in high school musicals for fun. Either way, there are a lot of things you can do to train your mind and body to continue to work as a dancer.

Taking Classes

Just because your show is over doesn't mean your experience with dance has to be. If dance is something that you are still interested in pursuing—professionally or recreationally—you should continue to enroll in classes. There are many different styles and skill levels that you can train in. Seeing as how most of your

Enrolling in classes—much like the ballet class seen here—is an ideal way to continue your involvement with dance, whether it is just for fun or for your professional goals.

experience will have likely been in jazz or ballet, you should branch out even further and take a modern class, a hip-hop class, an Afro-Caribbean class, a salsa class, a ballroom class, a swing class, a tap class, or a lyrical class. The more well-rounded you are in terms of your training, the easier you will find auditions and rehearsals.

Finding a Dance Coach

If you are still insecure about your dancing abilities and truly feel that a class setting isn't the right option for you at this point, some studios offer individual coaching. Schedule a few one-on-one sessions with a teacher and learn the basics. However, you will grow much faster as a dancer if you are in classes with others. Individual lessons are beneficial, but make the move to a classroom setting as soon as you are comfortable.

Summer Programs

Another ideal way to further your training is to attend a summer dance program. There are several factors in deciding which type of program will be best for you. Here are some good tips to make sure you get into the program you want:

- Determine if you would rather attend a day program or an overnight program.
- Contact your local dance studio and ask if it provides or recommends summer camp programs for different experience levels. Also, consider a more general performing arts camp that offers dance as a daily elective. You should also be aware that local colleges often offer summer programs. You can get more information by contacting the fine arts department of the college.
- Enroll early because many programs often have waiting lists. Cancellations always occur, so as summer nears, contact the program that interests you and see if it has any openings.

Your Career as a Choreographer

If you wish to continue your work as a choreographer, the options listed above are ideal for your continued growth. In addition, you will want to continue expanding your knowledge of dance.

Attend Dance Concerts

Your goal as a choreographer is to bring creative, inventive, and effective movement to the show you are working on. Therefore, the more types of dance that you are exposed to, the wider your range of choreography options are. No matter what style you choreograph in, movement from other genres can easily be adapted to your work.

Taking a dance class is not only beneficial to your training, but it also serves as a great way to keep your body active and healthy.

Workshop

Just as there are dance camps available, there are also choreography workshops. These workshops often include guest lecturers, discussion series, performances, and the opportunity to set your own choreography on dancers. Places where you can attend these

Choreographers should always have a notebook handy. You never know when inspiration or ideas for your choreography may strike. You'll want to remember them when you start creating steps.

workshops range from dance studios to summer programs at colleges.

Your Notebook

Many choreographers keep a notebook with them in order to write

down their ideas when inspiration strikes. You can also watch music videos, movie musicals, and dance concerts and write down what moves or elements of style you liked and how you would blend those into your own pieces. Study choreographers whose work you identify with—and even those you don't. Note why you love what you are seeing, or why you don't. The more specific you can be in your

Dance Pioneers

The following are a group of some of the greatest dancers and choreographers of all time. As you continue to grow as a dancer or choreographer, be sure to check out some of the pioneers and study their techniques!

- **George Balanchine** A pioneer of American ballet and ballet master of the New York City Ballet.
- **Mikhail Baryshnikov** A Russian American dancer, choreographer, and actor hailed as one of the greatest ballet dancers of the twentieth century.
- **Suzanne Farrell** One of the most famous ballerinas of the twentieth century and founder of the Suzanne Farrell Ballet.
- **Anna Pavlova** A Russian ballerina in the late nineteenth and early twentieth century who is credited with introducing ballet to many parts of the world that had never been exposed to it before.
- **Marius Petipa** A Russian choreographer and ballet master who has been heralded as one of the most influential ballet figures of all time.
- **Jack Cole** An American choreographer and director known as the "Father of Theatrical Jazz Dance."
- **Katherine Dunham** An American jazz and modern choreographer and anthropologist who created the Dunham Technique.
- **Bob Fosse** One of the most influential jazz choreographers and directors of all time. His style includes movements like inward knees, rounded shoulders, and body isolations.
- **Gus Giordano** One of the founders of jazz dance and the author of *Anthology of American Jazz Dance*, the first book on jazz dance.
- **Jerome Robbins** A film director and choreographer who worked in mediums from classical ballet to contemporary musical theater.

- **Alvin Ailey** A modern dance choreographer who founded the Alvin Ailey American Dance Theater.
- **Merce Cunningham** A dancer and controversial choreographer who founded the Merce Cunningham Dance Company.
- **Ruth St. Denis** A modern dance pioneer who founded one of the first dance departments at an American university (Adelphi University).
- **Isadora Duncan** A dancer who has been called the "Mother of Modern Dance" whose bizarre death has, at times, overshadowed her actual contributions to the genre.
- **Loie Fuller** A pioneer of modern dance and theater lighting techniques.
- **Martha Graham** A dancer and choreographer who has been regarded as the foremost pioneer of modern dance.
- **Ted Shawn** One of the first noted male pioneers of modern dance and along with his wife, Ruth St. Denis, created an acclaimed dance school named Denishawn.
- **Brenda Bufalino** A world renowned tap dancer, teacher, and choreographer.
- **The Nicholas Brothers** Brothers who were hailed as the greatest tap dancers of their day due to their artistry and innovation.

The Martha Graham Dance Company was founded in 1926 by Martha Graham *(shown here)* and is one of the most respected dance companies in the world.

writing, the easier it will be for you to have a reference point when choreographing.

We have looked at ways to help prepare you for your audition, how to nail your audition, what to expect and how to navigate through your rehearsals, your opening night, and the ways you can ready yourself. You have also looked at what a choreographer needs to do in order to take a show from the blueprint stage to the theatrical stage. Whether you aspire to continue participating in theater after high school or you have your sights set on other dreams that you want to achieve, the experience of a high school musical will teach you many lessons that can only benefit your future plans. You will learn to work in a group, to be professional, to be prepared, and to be committed. So, keep in mind all that you have read, and get ready, because the curtain is about to go up on your very own high school musical!

characterization The process of conveying information about characters.

choreography The art of creating and arranging dances.

ensemble A group of dancers performing together in the same production.

foundation The basic principles of a discipline, such as dance, that can be built upon.

grand battement An exercise in which the working leg is raised from the hip into the air and brought down again.

improvisation Movement that is created spontaneously, ranging from free form to highly structured, but is always highlighting the element of chance.

jazz shoe Similar in basic structure to a split-sole ballet slipper, jazz shoes usually have a longer vamp, securing the foot by laces or elastic inserts.

leotard A skin-tight, one-piece garment that covers the torso and upper body but leaves the legs free for movement.

opening-night jitters The fear, excitement, and nervousness that a performer feels before going onstage for the first time.

percussion The sound caused by the striking together of two objects.

pirouette A full turn on the toe or ball of one foot in ballet.

placement The correct positioning of the body (torso, legs, head, arms, hands) in ballet.

plié A bending of the knees outward by a ballet dancer with the back held straight.

pointe Ballet dancing that is performed on the tip of the toes.

run-through A performance of a show from start to finish without an audience.

stage manager Someone who supervises the physical aspects in the production of a show and who is in charge while the show is being performed.

syncopation A temporary displacement of the regular metrical accent in music caused typically by stressing the weak beat.

turnout The rotation of a dancer's legs from the hip sockets in classical ballet.

American Alliance for Health, Physical Education, Recreation and Dance

1900 Association Drive
Reston, VA 20191-1598
(703) 476-3400
Web site: http://www.aahperd.org/NDA
This alliance leads in promoting and supporting creative, artistic, and healthy lifestyles through quality services and programs in dance and dance education.

Broadway Theatre Project

2780 East Fowler Avenue
Tampa, FL 33612
(888) 874-1764
Web site: http://broadwaytheatreproject.com
The BTP is a three-week intensive program open to high school and college students that provides training from working professionals in film, television, and theater.

Canada Council for the Arts

350 Albert Street
P.O. Box 1047
Ottawa, ON K1P 5V8
Canada
(800) 263-5588
Web site: http://www.canadacouncil.ca

The Canada Council for the Arts supports, promotes, and celebrates the work of Canadian artists and arts organizations, including dance, music, and theater.

Drama Book Shop, Inc.
250 West 40th Street
New York, NY 10018
(212) 944-0595
Web site: http://www.dramabookshop.com
This renowned bookstore offers online ordering of plays, sheet music, and other books related to the performing arts.

Interlochen Center for the Arts
P.O. Box 199
Interlochen, MI 49643-0199
(231) 276-7200
Web site: http://www.interlochen.org
Interlochen is a performing arts boarding school that also offers summer programs in the visual and performing arts.

Martha Graham Center of Contemporary Dance
316 East 63rd Street
New York, NY 10065
(212) 838.5886
Web site: http://marthagraham.org/center
The Martha Graham Center of Contemporary Dance is the oldest, most celebrated modern dance company in the world.

Musical Theatre International
421 West 54th Street

New York, NY 10019
(212) 541-4684
Web site: http://www.mtishows.com
MTI has taken a leading role in theater education by creating the MTI
Theatrical Resources, a "theatrical tool box" designed to help not
only ensure the success of each musical production but also to
establish the study of musical theater as a permanent part of the
high school curriculum.

Teens@The Turn
The Citadel Theatre
9828–101A Avenue
Edmonton, AB T5J 3C6
Canada
(780) 425-1820
Web site: http://www.citadeltheatre.com/teens/index.php
Teens@The Turn provides professional mentorship and production
opportunities for teen playwrights, actors/dancers, directors,
designers, and stage managers.

Web Sites

Due to the changing nature of Internet links, Rosen Publishing has
developed an online list of Web sites related to the subject of this
book. This site is updated regularly. Please use this link to access
the list:

http://www.rosenlinks.com/hsm/danc

Bloom, Ken, and Frank Vlastnik. *Broadway Musicals: The 101 Greatest Shows of All Time.* New York, NY: Black Dog & Leventhal Publishers, 2008.

Bryer, Jackson R. *The Art of the American Musical: Conversations with the Creators.* Piscataway, NJ: Rutgers University Press, 2005.

Filichia, Peter. *Let's Put on a Musical! How to Choose the Right Show for Your School, Community, or Professional Theater.* New York, NY: Watson-Guptill Publications, 2004.

Gottfried, Martin. *All His Jazz: The Life and Death of Bob Fosse.* Cambridge, MA: De Capo Books, 2003.

Grant, Gail. *Technical Manual and Dictionary of Classical Ballet.* Mineola, NY: Dover Books, 1982.

Hatchett, Frank, and Nancy Myers Giltin. *Frank Hatchett's Jazz Dance.* Champaign, IL: Human Kinetics Publishers, 2000.

Kraines, Minda Goodman, and Esther Pyror. *Jump Into Jazz: The Basics and Beyond for Jazz Students.* Columbus, OH: McGraw-Hill Humanities/Social Sciences/Languages, 2004.

Eichenbaum, Rose. *Masters of Movement: Portraits of America's Greatest Choreographers*. Washington, DC: Smithsonian Books, 2007.

Franklin, Eric. *Conditioning for Dance*. Champaign, IL: Human Kinetics Publishers, 2003.

Hischak, Thomas S. *The Oxford Companion to the American Musical: Theatre, Film, and Television*. New York, NY: Oxford University Press, 2008.

Linklater, Kristen. *Freeing the Natural Voice*. London, England: Quite Specific Media Group, 1988.

Roseman, Janet L. *Dance Masters: Interviews with Legends of Dance*. New York, NY: Routledge, 2001.

Sofras, Pamela. *Dance Composition Basics: Capturing the Choreographer's Craft*. Champaign, IL: Human Kinetics Publishers, 2006.

INDEX

A

Afro-Caribbean dance, 46
Ailey, Alvin, 53
Anthology of American Jazz Dance, 52

B

Balanchine, George, 52
ballet, 6, 7, 30, 46, 48, 52
ballroom dance, 46
Baryshnikov, Mikhail, 52
Bufalino, Brenda, 53

C

cast recordings, original, 10
characterizations, 31, 33, 42
choreographers
   conducting auditions, 18–20
   conducting rehearsals, 21–24,
      25–26, 28, 30–33, 54
   opening-night prep for, 39–42, 44
   and song choices, 10, 19, 26
choreography
   as a career, 48, 50–51, 54
   pioneers of, 52–53
Cole, Jack, 52
Cunningham, Merce, 53

D

dance
   bags, 27
   classes, 7–8, 45–47
   clothing, 12–13
   coaches, 47
   joys of, 4, 34, 38
   pioneers of, 52–53
   studios, 8, 47, 48, 51
   summer programs, 47–48
dancers
   and costumes, 29, 44
   dealing with nervousness, 11, 13,
      15, 18, 36–38, 44
   expressing emotion/energy, 4, 18,
      24, 28, 31, 33, 42
   learning choreography, 15–18,
      21–23, 31, 37–38
   preparing for auditions, 7–18, 46
   and rehearsals, 21–24, 27, 46, 54
dress codes, 12, 28
Duncan, Isadora, 53
Dunham, Katherine, 52

E

eight-count steps, 16–17, 19

F

Farrell, Suzanne, 52
Fosse, Bob, 4, 52
Fuller, Loie, 53

G

Giordano, Gus, 52
Graham, Martha, 53
grand battements, 44

H

high school musicals
    auditions for, 6–13, 15–20
    crews of, 12, 19, 26, 38–39, 44
    vs. filmed versions, 9
    and friendships, 5, 23–24
    leading to a theater career, 4–5, 45,
       48, 50–51
    and opening night, 34, 36–42, 44
    rehearsals for, 21–24, 26–28, 30–33
hip-hop dance, 6, 46

I

improvisation, 7

J

jazz dance, 6, 7, 28, 46, 48, 52
jazz shoes, buying, 12, 13

L

leotards, buying, 12
lyrical dance, 46

M

Mattox, Matt, 7
modern dance, 6, 7, 48, 52, 53

N

New York City Ballet, 52
Nicholas Brothers, 53
nonverbal communication,
    effectiveness of, 4

O

opening-night jitters, 38

P

Pavlova, Anna, 52
percussion, 7
Petipa, Marius, 52
pirouettes, 20
pliés, 30
pointe work, 6

R

rehearsal space vs. stage space, 42, 44
Robbins, Jerome, 52
run-throughs, 39–42, 44

S

salsa dance, 46
Shawn, Ted, 53
stage traffic patterns, 40–42
St. Denis, Ruth, 53
swing dance, 46
syncopation, 7

T

tap dance, 6, 7, 30, 46, 53
time management tips, 30–33
turnout, 6

W

warm-up exercises, 15, 28, 30, 34

About the Author

Michael Joosten is a graduate of Boston's Emerson College and holds a BFA in musical theater. He currently lives in New York City, performs in various musicals and cabarets, and writes for young adults.

Photo Credits

Cover (background), p. 1 Hans Neleman/Taxi/Getty Images; cover (inset) Michael Kemp/Rubberball Productions/Getty Images; pp. 4–5 Andrew H. Walker/Getty Images; pp. 8–9 © Gaetan Bally/Keystone/Corbis; pp. 10–11 © Julia Cumes/Syracuse Newspapers/The Image Works; p. 14 © moodboard/Corbis; pp. 16–17 © Gloria Wright/Syracuse Newspapers/The Image Works; pp. 22–23 © Arnold Gold/New Haven Register/The Image Works; p. 25 © Jim West/The Image Works; pp. 27, 50–51 Shutterstock.com; p. 29 Win-Initiative/Getty Images; pp. 32–33 Spencer Platt/Getty Images; p. 35 © ArenaPal/Topham/The Image Works; pp. 36–37 © Peter Chen/Syracuse Newspapers/The Image Works; pp. 40–41 © Peter Hvizdak/The Image Works; p. 43 Digital Vision/Getty Images; pp. 46–47 © David Turnley/Corbis; p. 49 © age fotostock/SuperStock; p. 53 Robin Jones/Hulton Archive/Getty Images.

Designer: Sam Zavieh; Editor: Bethany Bryan
Photo Researcher: Cindy Reiman